BUCKINGHAMSHIRE
Wit & Humour

RICHIE VILLIERS

BRADWELL
BOOKS

Published by Bradwell Books
9 Orgreave Close Sheffield S13 9NP
Email: books@bradwellbooks.co.uk
Compiled by Richie Villiers

All rights reserved. No part of this publication may be reproduced, stored in a retrieval system or transmitted in any form or by any means, electronic, mechanical, photocopying, recording or otherwise without the prior permission of Bradwell Books.

British Library Cataloguing in Publication Data: a catalogue record for this book is available from the British Library.

1st Edition

ISBN: 9781909914643

Print: Gomer Press, Llandysul, Ceredigion SA44 4JL
Design by: jenksdesign@yahoo.co.uk/07506 471162
Illustrations: ©Tim O'Brien 2014

At a primary school in Stokenchurch, the teacher came up with a good problem for her maths class to solve.

"Suppose, there were a dozen sheep and six of them jumped over a fence," she said to the group of seven-year-olds, "How many would be left?"

Little Harry, a farmer's son, put his hand up. "None," he answered.

"None?" exclaimed his teacher. "Harry, I'm afraid you don't know your arithmetic."

"Really, Miss?" said Harry, cockily, "And you don't know your sheep. When one goes, they all go!"

A gang of robbers broke into the Aylesbury Lawyers' Club by mistake. The old legal lions put up a fierce fight for their lives and their money. The gang was happy to escape in one piece. "It ain't so bad," one crook said. "At least we got fifty quid between us."

His boss screamed at him, "I warned you to stay clear of lawyers... we had 200 quid when we broke in!"

Why couldn't the lifeguard save the hippie?

He was too far out, man!

At a cricket match in Amersham, a fast bowler sent one down and it just clipped the bail. As nobody yelled "Ow's att", the batsman picked up the bail and replaced it. He looked at the umpire and said, "Windy today isn't it?"

"Yes," said the umpire, "Mind it doesn't blow your cap off when you're walking back to the pavilion."

A Buckinghamshire man is driving through Berkshire, when he passes a farmer standing in the middle of a huge field. He pulls the car over and watches the farmer standing stock-still, doing absolutely nothing. Intrigued, the man walks over to the farmer and asks him, "Excuse me sir, but what are you doing?"

The farmer replies, "I'm trying to win a Nobel Prize."

"How?" Asks the puzzled Buckinghamshire man.

"Well," says the farmer, "I heard they give the prize to people who are outstanding in their field."

BUCKINGHAMSHIRE Wit & Humour

A lady works in Milton Keynes and everyday she walks past a pet shop. One day she notices a parrot in the window and stops to admire the bird. The parrot says to her, "Alright, love? You're a great big ugly moo."

Well, the lady is furious! She storms off but, on her way back from work, she passes the same parrot and, when it sees her, the bird says, "Alright, love? You're a great big ugly moo."

She is incredibly angry now so she goes to the manager and threatens to sue the pet shop. She demands to have the bird put down. The manager apologises profusely and promises that the bird won't say it again. The next day, she decides to go back and check. She walks past the parrot and, when it sees her, it says, "Alright, love?"

The woman stops, scowls and with an icy stare, says, "Yes?"

The parrot struts back and forth on its perch in a cocky manner gawping at her, then it says, "You know."

Supporters, waiting to watch The Dons play Slough Town, heard that the Slough players were going to be delayed. They saw a sign on the M1 that said 'Clean Lavatories'... so they did.

The Dons beat Slough Town five – nothing; they were lucky to get nothing.

A high-rise building was going up in Milton Keynes and three steel erectors sat on a girder having their lunch.

"Oh, no, not cheese and pickle again," said Jim, the first one, "If I get the same again tomorrow, I'll jump off the girder."

Harry opened his packet. "Oh, no, not a chicken salad with mayo and lettuce on granary," he said. "If I get the same again tomorrow, I'll jump off too."

Owen, the third man, opened his lunch. "Oh, no, not another potato sandwich," he said. "If I get the same again tomorrow, I'll follow you two off the girder."

The next day, Jim got cheese and pickle. Without delay, he jumped. Harry saw he had chicken salad with mayo and lettuce

BUCKINGHAMSHIRE Wit & Humour

on granary, and with a wild cry, he leapt too. Then the third man, Owen, opened his lunchbox. "Oh, no," he said. "Potato sandwiches." And he too jumped.

The foreman, who had overheard their conversation, reported what had happened, and the funerals were held together.

"If only I'd known," sobbed Jim's wife.

"If only he'd said," wailed Harry's wife.

"I don't understand it at all," said Owen's wife. "He always got his own sandwiches ready."

The magistrate at Aylesbury County Court spoke sharply to the defendant, "But if you saw the lady driving towards you, why didn't you give her half the road?"

"I was going to, your Honour," replied the motorist, "…as soon as I could work out which half she wanted."

There's a man in Windsor who claims to have invented a game that's a bit like cricket; what he doesn't realise is Berkshire County Cricket Club's been playing it for years.

A passenger in a taxi tapped the driver on the shoulder to ask him something.

The driver screamed, lost control of the cab, nearly hit a bus, drove up over the curb and stopped just inches from a large plate glass window.

For a few moments everything was silent in the cab, then the driver said, "Please, don't ever do that again. You scared the daylights out of me."

The passenger, who was also frightened, apologised and said he didn't realise that a tap on the shoulder could frighten him so much, to which the driver replied, "I'm sorry, it's really not your fault at all. Today is my first day driving a cab. I've been driving a hearse for the last twenty-five years."

A group of backpackers from the Buckinghamshire New University were sitting around a campfire one evening when a stranger asked to join them. Glad to add to their group, they agreed. The evening's fun soon turned to jokes. One of the students started to tell jokes in which Reading Uni was the butt of the humour. The stranger who, it turned out, had graduated from University of Reading himself, became more and more furious with each quip. Finally, he had had enough and pulled out his razor and began to threaten the Buckinghamshire lads with it. Fortunately for them, he couldn't find a socket to plug it into.

A plain Jane from Bletchley goes to see Madame Grizelda, a fortune-teller, and asks about her future love life.

Madame Grizelda tells her, "Two men are madly in love with you – Mark and Maurice."

"Who will be the lucky one?" asks Jane excitedly.

Madame Grizelda answers, "Maurice will marry you, and Mark will be the lucky one."

Fred's wife has been missing for over a week. The police liaison officer warned him to prepare for the worst…so Fred went to the charity shop to get all her clothes back.

A man from Stony Stratford man decided to become a monk so he went to the monastery and talked to the head monk. The head monk said, "You must take a vow of silence and can only say two words every three years."

The man agreed and after the first three years, the head monk came to him and said, "What are your two words?"

"Food cold!" the man replied.

Three more years went by and the head monk came to him and said, "What are your two words?"

"Robe dirty!" the man exclaimed. Three more years went by and the head monk came to him and said, "What are your two words?"

"I quit!" said the man.

"Well," the head monk replied, "I'm not surprised. You've done nothing but complain ever since you got here!"

Q: What did one ocean say to the other ocean?
A: Nothing, they just waved.

Down the King's Head, a group of blokes sit around drinking when a mobile phone on the table rings. One of the men picks up the mobile and puts the speaker-phone on.

A woman's voice says, "How are you, darling? I hope you don't mind but I've just seen a diamond ring priced £2000 and wondered if I can buy it? I've got your credit card with me."

"Of course, my dear, go ahead," answers the man.

"While I'm on," purrs the lady, "I've noticed a top of the range car I'd like. It's only £65,000, could I order that as well?"

"Of course, my angel," replies the man.

His friends around the table look at each other in disbelief as the lady continues, "And I've just noticed a lovely house on the coast, lover. It's only £750,000 - could we have that as well please?"

"Of course, sugar," answers the man, without so much as blinking.

The phone call is ended and the man smiles at the others and takes a long swill of beer. Then he looks around and shouts "Anyone know whose phone this is?"

Two blokes are standing in the Milton Keynes Job Centre, waiting for their turn at the counter.

The first bloke says to the second one, "I have to buy my wife something nice for our wedding anniversary and the benefits cheque won't cover it."

The second bloke looks up from his paper and says, "What date?"

The first bloke thinks for a while and says, "15th September."

The second bloke considers his next question. "What year?"

Without taking a breath, the first bloke replies, "Every year for the last twenty-seven!"

A Bletchley man fell out with his in-laws and banned them from entering the house while he was in it. His wife faithfully carried out his wishes until she was on her death bed and then asked sadly, "Haven't I always been a supportive wife to you, John?"

"Yes, my dear," he replied, "The best."

"Then I would love it if you could grant my last request and let my sister Sarah ride in the first car with you at my funeral?"

"Alright, my dear," he agreed heavily, "But I'm warning you, it'll spoil all my pleasure!"

Two council workers on a site in Aylesbury are surveying land they're about to dig up.

The gaffer says to one of them, "You go and get the metal detector and check for pipe work and I'll get the kettle on and have a brew."

The gaffer gets the tea going while his mate starts work. Half-hour later the gaffer puts his paper down, next to his mug of tea, to find out how work is progressing and he finds his mate sitting on a wall scratching his head.

"What's up with you?" The gaffer asks. "There's pipework all over the place. Look!"

The young worker sets off across the land, the bleeper sounding continuously as the detector passes in front of him

The gaffer watches him, laughing, then he says, "Are you soft or what? You've got steel toe caps in your boots!"

It was match day for the 'Dons' and excited crowds filled the streets of Milton Keynes, heading for the stadium. A funeral procession drove slowly through the throng. One of the Milton Keynes. supporters stopped, took off his hat and bowed reverently as the hearse passed.

"That was a nice thing to do," remarked his mate.

"Well," said the 'Dons' fan, "She was a good wife to me for thirty odd years."

Q: What's the difference between a new husband and a new dog?
A: After a year, the dog is still excited to see you.

Two Dinton Cricket Club players are chatting in the bar after a match. "So did you have a hard time explaining last week's game to the wife?" says one.

"I certainly did, "says the other," She found out I wasn't there!"

Derek and Duncan were long-time neighbours in Chalfont St. Peter. Every time, Derek saw Duncan coming round to his house, his heart sank. This was because he knew that, as always, Duncan would be visiting him in order to borrow something and he was fed up with it.

"I'm not going to let Duncan get away with it this time," he said quietly to his wife, "Watch what I'm about to do."

"Hi there, I wondered if you were thinking about using your hedge trimmer this afternoon?" asked Duncan.

"Oh, I'm very sorry," said Derek, trying to look apologetic, "but I'm actually going to be using it all afternoon."

"In that case," replied Duncan with a big grin, "You won't be using your golf clubs, will you? Mind if I borrow them?"

Three Buckinghamshire women are talking in a bar about a party they've been invited to.

The first one says, "We've got to all wear an item that matches something belonging to our husbands at this party, haven't we?"

"Yeah," said the other two, "But what?"

The first one continued, "Well, my husband's got black hair and I've got a little black dress I can diet into by then."

The second one says, "That's a good idea. My husband has got brown hair and I've got a brown dress I can diet into by then too."

The third one looks a bit hesitant and says, "I just need to go on a diet - my husband's bald!"

"You're looking glum," the captain of Boyn Hill Cricket Club remarked to one of his players.

"Yes, the doctor says I can't play cricket," said the downcast man.

"Really?" replied the captain, "I didn't know he'd ever seen you play?"

Darren proudly drove his new convertible into Beaconsfield and parked it on the main street. He was on his way to the recycling centre to get rid of an unwanted gift, a foot spa, which he left on the back seat.

He had walked half way down the street when he realised that he had left the top down with the foot spa still in the back. He ran all the way back to his car, but it was too late...another five foot spas had been dumped in the car.

Ten women out on a hen night in Aylesbury thought it would be sensible if one of them stayed more sober than the other nine and looked after the money to pay for their drinks. After deciding who would hold the money, they all put twenty pounds into the kitty to cover expenses. At closing time after a few white wine spritzers, several vodka and cokes, and a Pina Colada each, they stood around deciding how to divvy up the leftover cash.

"How do we stand?" said Sharon.

"Stand?!" said Debbie. "That's the easy part! I'm wondering how I can walk. I've missed the last bus to Wendover!"

A lawyer at Aylesbury Crown Court says to the judge, "Your Honour, I wish to appeal my client's case on the basis of newly discovered evidence."

His Lordship replies, "And what is the nature of the new evidence?"

The lawyer says, "My Lord, I discovered that my client still has £500 left."

A pupil at a school in Aylesbury asked his teacher, "Are 'trousers' singular or plural?"

The teacher replied, "They're singular on top and plural on the bottom."

One afternoon at Buckinghamshire New University, a group of freshers, who had just started their psychology course, were attending one of their first seminars. The topic was emotional extremes.

"Let's begin by discussing some contrasts," said the tutor. He pointed to a student in the front row, "What is the opposite of joy?"

The student thought about it briefly, then answered "Sadness." The tutor asked another student, "What is the opposite of depression?"

She paused then said, "Elation."

"And you," the tutor said to another student sitting at the back, "What about the opposite of woe?"

The student thought for a moment, then replied, "Um, I believe that would be 'giddy up'."

A man rushed into Amersham Hospital and asked a nurse for a cure for hiccups. Grabbing a cup of water, the nurse quickly splashed it into the man's face.

"What did you that for?" screamed the man, wiping his face.
"Well, you don't have the hiccups now, do you?" said the nurse.
"No," replied the man. "But my wife out in the car does.

"Dad," says the little boy, "Can I play football with the lads in the street?"

"No," says his dad, "They swear too much."

"But you play with them, Dad?"

"I swear already."

A woman walked into the kitchen to find her husband stalking around with a fly swatter. "What are you doing?" She demanded.

"Hunting flies," he replied.

"Oh. Killed any?" She asked.

"Yep, three males and two females," he replied."

Intrigued, she said, "How can you tell?"

"Three were on a beer can, and two were on the phone," he replied.

Sam worked in a telephone marketing company in Aylesbury. One day he walked into his boss's office and said, "I'll be honest with you, I know the economy isn't great, but I have three companies after me, and, with respect, I would like to ask for a pay rise."

After a few minutes of haggling, his manager finally agreed to a 5% pay rise, and Sam happily got up to leave.

"By the way," asked the boss as Sam went to the door, "which three companies are after you?"

"The electric company, the water company, and the phone company," Sam replied.

BUCKINGHAMSHIRE Wit & Humour

A driver pulls up by a traffic warden in the middle of High Wycombe.

"If I park on these double yellow lines and pop over the road to post a letter will you give me a ticket?" asks the driver.

"Of course, I will," replied the warden.

"But these other cars are parked on double yellow lines," argues the driver looking around him.

"I know," replied the warden. "but they didn't ask me to give them a ticket."

In a school in Denham, a little boy just wasn't getting good marks. One day, his teacher was checking his homework and said, "Lee, once again I'm afraid I can only give you two out of ten."

Little Lee looked up at her and said, "Well, Miss, I don't want to scare you, but…"

He stopped, a worried expression on his face.

"What is it? Tell me, Lee," said his teacher kindly.

"Well," said the boy, "my daddy says if I don't get better marks soon, somebody is going to get a spanking."

An estate agent parks his beautifully restored E-type Jag in front of the office in Bedford to show it off to his colleagues. As he's getting out of the car, a truck comes along, takes off the door and the driver carries on oblivious to the damage he has wreaked.

More than a little distraught, the estate agent grabs his mobile and calls the police. Five minutes later, the police arrive. Before the policeman has a chance to ask any questions, the estate agent starts screaming hysterically:

"My Jag, my beautiful beautiful Jag is ruined, it'll simply never be the same again!"

After the estate agent finally finishes his rant, the policeman shakes his head in disgust, "I can't believe how materialistic you estate agents are,"

"You lot are so focused on your possessions that you don't notice anything else in your life."

"How can you say such a thing at a time like this?" snaps the estate agent.

The policeman replies, "Didn't you realise that your right arm was torn off when the truck hit you?"

The estate agent looks down in absolute horror…

"Oh my goodness!" he screams, "Where's my Rolex?!"

A farmer was driving along a country road near the village of Quainton with a large load of fertiliser. A little boy, playing in front of his house, saw him and called out, "What do you have on your truck?"

"Fertiliser," the farmer replied.

"What are you going to do with it?" asked the little boy.

"Put it on strawberries," answered the farmer.

"You ought to live here," the little boy advised him. "We put sugar and cream on ours."

BUCKINGHAMSHIRE Wit & Humour

An old bloke at the bus stop outside Wycombe Hospital is talking to the next person in the queue whilst rubbing his head.

"My wooden leg ain't half giving me some gyp," complained the old boy.

The person in the queue looks at him, wondering why he keeps rubbing his head, and says, "Really? Why?"

The old man retorted, "Cos my missus keeps hitting me over the head with it!"

Phil's nephew came to him with a problem. "I have my choice of two women," he said, with a worried frown, "A beautiful, penniless young girl whom I love dearly, and a rich widow who I don't really love."

"Follow your heart," Phil counselled, "marry the girl you love."

"Very well, Uncle Phil," said the nephew, "That's sound advice. Thank you."

"You're welcome," replied Phil with a smile, "by the way, where does the widow live?"

A tramp walks into a pub in Chesham and asks the barman for a drink. The barman looks at the shabby, impoverished-looking tramp and refuses. The tramp says, "If I show you what I've got in my pocket and you agree that it's fantastic, can I have that drink?" The barman agrees whereupon the tramp takes a hamster out of his pocket and puts him on the bar. The hamster runs along the bar and over to the piano where he begins playing Gershwin melodies. Amazed, the barman gives the tramp his drink. Ten minutes later the tramp asks for another drink and the barman refuses until the tramp makes a similar offer. This time he takes a frog out of his pocket and puts him on the bar. The frog sings like Pavarotti accompanied by the hamster on the piano. At that moment, a chap in the corner of the bar rushes up to the tramp and offers him £500 for the frog. The tramp accepts and the chap pays up and rushes out of the bar. As the barman is serving the tramp with his second drink, he says, "You must be mad. That frog is worth millions!"

"I don't think so," replies the tramp, "the hamster's a ventriloquist!!"

One Sunday in St Mary's church, in Addington, the vicar opened his Bible and began to read the lesson. In a loud voice, he proclaimed, "Corinthians 7."

A keen Aylesbury F.C. fan, who had been dozing in the front pew, woke up with a start and shouted out, "Blimey! Who were they playing?"

A farmer from Berkshire once visited a farmer based near Granborough. The visitor asked, "How big is your farm?" to which the Buckinghamshire farmer replied, "Can you see those trees over there? That's the boundary of my farmland".

"Is that all?" said the Berkshire farmer, "It takes me three days to drive to the boundary of my farm."

The Granborough man looked at him and said, "I had a car like that once."

One day at Stoke Mandeville Hospital, a group of primary school children were being given a tour. A nurse showed them the x-ray machines and asked them if they had ever had broke a bone.

One little boy raised his hand, "I did!"

"Did it hurt?" the nurse asked.

"No!" he replied.

"Wow, you must be a very brave boy!" said the nurse. "What did you break?"

"My sister's arm!"

The nervous young batsman playing for Waddesdon Cricket Club was having a very bad day. In a quiet moment in the game, he muttered to the one of his team mates, "Well, I suppose you've seen worse players."

There was no response…so he said it again, "I said 'I guess you've seen worse players.'"

His team mate looked at him and answered, "I heard you the first time. I was just trying to think…"

When the manager of Slough Town started to tell the team about tactics, half the players thought he was talking about a new kind of peppermint.

A woman from Marlow called Mandy was still not married at thirty-five and she was getting really tired of going to family weddings especially because her old Aunt Maud always came over and said, "You're next!"

It made Mandy so annoyed she racked her brains to figure out how to get Aunt Maud to stop.

Sadly, an old uncle died and there was a big family funeral. Mandy spotted Aunt Maud in the crematorium, walked over, pointed at the coffin and said, with a big smile, "You're next!"

A man and his wife walked past a swanky new restaurant in Chalfont St. Giles. "Did you smell that food?" the woman asked. "Wonderful!"

Being the kind-hearted, generous man that he was, her husband thought, "What the heck, I'll treat her!"

So they walked past it a second time.

Peter walked up to the sales lady in the clothing department of a large shop in High Wycombe.

"I would like to buy my wife a pretty pair of tights," he said. "Something cute with love-hearts or flower patterns."

"Oh, that's so sweet," exclaimed the sales lady, "I'll bet she'll be really surprised." "I'll say," said Peter, "she's expecting a new diamond ring!"

For a minute Slough Town were in with a chance – then the game started.

Did you hear about the last wish of the henpecked husband of a house-proud wife?

He asked to have his ashes scattered on the carpet.

An expectant father rang the Stoke Mandeville Maternity Wing to see how his wife, who had gone into labour, was getting on. By mistake, he was connected to the Buckinghamshire County Cricket ground.

"How's it going?" he asked.

"Fine." came the answer, "We've got three out and hope to have the rest out before lunch. The last one was a duck."

What do you get if you cross the Slough Town with an OXO cube?
A laughing stock.

Resolving to surprise her husband, an investment banker's wife from Gerrards Cross pops by his office in the City. She finds him with his secretary sitting in his lap. Without hesitation, he starts dictating, "…and in conclusion, gentlemen, credit crunch or no credit crunch, I cannot continue to operate this office with just one chair!"

Patient: "Doctor, doctor! I've broken my arm in a couple of places!"

Doctor: "Then stay away from those places!"

Pete and Larry hadn't seen each other in many years. They were having a long chat, telling each other all about their lives. Finally Pete invited Larry to visit him in his new flat in Milton Keynes. "I have a wife and three kids and I'd love to have you visit us."

"Great. Where do you live?"

"Here's the address. There's plenty of parking behind the flat. Park and come around to the front door, kick it open with your foot, go to the lift and press the button with your left elbow, then enter! When you reach the sixth floor, go down the hall until you see my name on the door. Then press the doorbell with your right elbow and I'll let you in."

"Great. But tell me...what is all this business of kicking the front door open, then pressing elevator buttons with my right, then my left elbow?"

Pete answered, "Surely you're not coming empty-handed?"

Patient: "Doctor, doctor! I keep thinking I'm a dog."

Doctor: "Please, take a seat."

Patient: "I'm not allowed on the furniture."

Anne and Matt, a local couple, went to the Buckinghamshire County Show and found a weighing scale that tells your fortune and weight.

"Hey, listen to this," said Matt, showing his wife a small white card. "It says I'm bright, energetic, and a great husband."

"Yeah," said Anna, "And it has your weight wrong too."

Three blondes were walking near the Wendover Woods when they came upon a set of tracks.

The first blonde said, "Those are deer tracks."

The second blonde said, "No, those are horse tracks."

The third blonde said, "You're both wrong, those are cattle tracks."

The Blondes were still arguing when the 11.20 to Marylebone hit them.

A labourer in Milton Keynes, shouted up to his roofer mate on top of an old terraced house, saying, "Don't start climbing down this ladder, Bert."

"Why not?" Bert called back.

"Cos I moved it five minutes ago!" replied his mate.

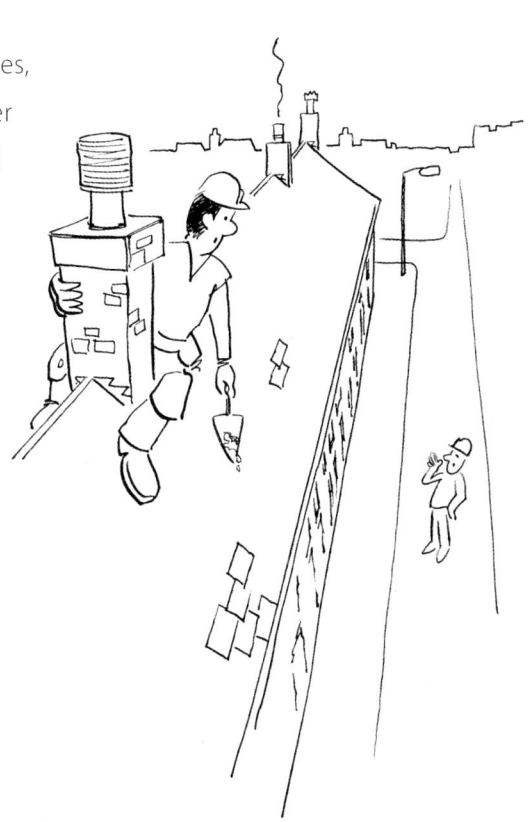

A Hurrah Henry from Berkshire was driving around Aylesbury in his fancy new car and realised that he was lost. The driver stopped a local character, old Tom, and said, "Hey, you there! Old man, what happens if I turn left here?"

"Don't know sir," replied Tom.

"Well, what if I turn right here - where will that take me?" continued the visitor.

"Don't know, sir," replied old Tom.

Becoming exasperated, the driver continued, "Well, what if I go straight on?"

A flicker of knowledge passed over old Tom's face but then he replied, "Don't know, sir."

"I say old man you don't know a lot do you?" retorted the posh bloke.

Old Tom looked at him and said, "I may not know a lot, sir, but I ain't lost like what you are!" With that, old Tom walked off leaving the motorist stranded.

An elderly husband and wife from Amersham visit their doctor when they begin forgetting little things. Their doctor tells them that many people find it useful to write themselves little notes.

When they get home, the wife says, "Dear, will you please go to the kitchen and get me a dish of ice cream? And maybe write that down so you won't forget?"

"Nonsense," says the husband, "I can remember a dish of ice cream."

"Well," says the wife, "I'd also like some strawberries and whipped cream on it."

"My memory's not all that bad," says the husband. "No problem - a dish of ice cream with strawberries and whipped cream. I don't need to write it down."

He goes into the kitchen; his wife hears pots and pans banging around. The husband finally emerges from the kitchen and presents his wife with a plate of bacon and eggs. She looks at the plate and asks, "Hey, where's the toast I asked for?"

A new dentist set up a surgery in Steeple Claydon and quickly acquired a reputation for being a "Painless" dentist. But soon a local chap disputed this.

"He's a fake!" he told his mates. "He's not painless at all. When he stuck his finger in my mouth I bit him - and he yelled like anyone else."

A Wendover housewife went to the greengrocer's. She picked up a lettuce and examined it. "Why is it that these iceberg lettuces just seem to be getting smaller and smaller?" she asked the shop assistant.

"Global warming," he replied.

An old chap from Maids Moreton went to the doctors.
"Doctor," says the old boy, "I feel really lousy, you know - under the weather."

"Flu?" asks the doc.
"No," says the old chap, "I rode here on my bike like I always do."

Two elderly ladies in Little Chalfont had been friends for many decades. Over the years, they had shared all kinds of fun but of late their activities had been limited to meeting a few times a week to play cards. One day, they were playing pontoon when one looked at the other and said, "Now don't get mad at me, my dear. I know we've been friends for a long time but I just can't think of your name. I've thought and thought, but I can't remember it. Please tell me what your name is." Her friend got a bit cross and, for at least three minutes, she just stared and glared at her. Finally she said, "How soon do you need to know?"

A reporter from The Bucks Herald was covering the local football league and went to see the Chalfont Wasps play Flackwell Heath. One of the Flackwell Heath players looked so old he went over to him and said, "You know you might be the oldest man playing in the league. How do you do it at your age?"

The man replied, "I drink six pints of lager every night, smoke two packets of fags a day, and eat tons of kebabs."

"Wow, that is incredible!" said the reporter, "How old did you say you were?"

"Twenty-two," said the player proudly

An elderly couple from Loudwater are sitting at the dining table in their semi-detached house talking about making preparations for writing their wills. Bill says to his missus, Edna, "I've been thinking, my dear, if I go first to meet me maker I don't want you to be on your own for too long. In fact, I think you could do worse than marry Colin in the Chemists or Dave with the fruit stall in the market. They'd provide for you and look after you when I'm gone."

"That's very kind on you to think about me like that, Bill," replied Edna, "But I've already made my own arrangements!"

An Ellesborough couple, Enid and Sidney, are having matrimonial difficulties and seek the advice of a counsellor. The couple are shown into a room where the counsellor asks Enid what problems, in her opinion, she faces in her relationship with Sidney.

"Well," she starts, "he shows me no affection, I don't seem to be important to him anymore. We don't share the same interests and I don't think he loves me at all." Enid has tears in her eyes as the counsellor walks over to her, gives her a big hug and kisses her firmly on the lips.

Sidney looks on in passive disbelief. The counsellor turns to Sidney and says, "This is what Enid needs once a day for the next month. Can you see that she gets it?"

Sidney looks unsettled, "Well I can drop her off everyday other than Wednesdays when I play snooker and Sundays when I go fishing!"

A policeman stops a drunk wandering the streets of Milton Keynes at four in the morning and says, "Can you explain why you are out at this hour, sir?"

The drunk replies, "If I was able to explain myself, I would have been home with the wife ages ago."

Two elderly ladies were enjoying a small sherry at home in Chalfont St. Peter.

One said to the other, "Was it love at first sight when you met your late husband?"

"No, I don't think so," came the reply, "I didn't know how much money he had when I first met him!"

A DEFRA Inspector goes to a small farm near Butler's Cross and knocks the door of the humble, tied cottage. A young boy opens the door and asks what business the man has on his parent's property.

"I've come to inspect the farm for compliance with EU regulations, my boy. Where's your father?"

"You can't speak to him, he's busy," says the surly child.

"I shall speak to him. He's had notice of my visit," the Inspector retorted firmly.

"Well, he's feeding the pigs at the moment," says the boy, "But you'll be able to tell me father easy enough - he's the one wearing a hat!"

A man from Princes Risborough said to his wife, "Get your coat on love. I'm off to the club".

His wife said, "That's nice. You haven't taken me out for years".

He said, "You're not coming with me...I'm turning the heating off when I go out".

A well-known academic from Reading University was giving a lecture on the philosophy of language at Buckinghamshire New University. He came to a curious aspect of English grammar.

"You will note," said the somewhat stuffy scholar, "That in the English language, two negatives can mean a positive, but it is never the case that two positives can mean a negative."

To which someone at the back responded, "Yeah, yeah."

A bloke from Stoke Poges goes into an artist's studio and asks if the artist could paint a picture of him surrounded by beautiful, scantily clad women. The artist agrees but he is intrigued by this strange request. He asks his new client why he wants such a picture painted and the bloke says, "Well, if I die before me missus when she finds this painting she'll wonder which one I spent all me money on!"

The next day the bloke's wife goes into the artist's studio and asks him to paint her wearing a big diamond necklace and matching earrings.

"Of course, madam," says the artist, "but may I ask why?"

"Well," replies the woman, "if I die before me husband I want his new woman to be frantic searching for all me jewellery!"

BUCKINGHAMSHIRE Wit & Humour

A couple from Woburn Sands had been courting for nearly twenty years. One day as they sat on a seat in the park, the woman plucked up the courage to ask, "Don't you think it's time we got married?" Her sweetheart answered, "Yes, but who'd have us?"